The Wit & Wisdom of
Benjamin Franklin

The Wit
& Wisdom of
Benjamin
Franklin

BARNES
&NOBLE
BOOKS
NEW YORK

Contents

Preface

L OVED BY AMERICANS EVERYWHERE, no other Founding Father has impressed himself in our culture as Benjamin Franklin has. Writer, scientist, diplomat, and philosopher, some of his noted accomplishments include starting the first American circulating library, inventing the Franklin stove, establishing the American Philosophical Society at Philadelphia, discovering the first law of electricity, and helping draft the Constitution.

The creator and personification of the American dream, Benjamin Franklin established and substantiated the belief that hard work and dedication would be justly rewarded. Born in 1706 to a poor Boston candlemaker and soap-boiler, Franklin had virtually no formal education. However, being a voracious reader he soon rose from a printer's apprentice to becoming a printer-publisher in his own right. By the time of his death in 1790, Franklin had become America's most revered political and literary figure.

Yet our images of the man are often confusing and paradoxical. Visions of a kindly, eccentric, grandfatherly character are often juxtaposed against those of a stern and puritanical parent. Perhaps it is because of this dichotomy in his personality and his unusual ability to merge this duality successfully that we honor Franklin as a mentor.

Through a generous sample of his work, this collection reveals the many facets of this whimsical yet critical writer. We discover the philosopher who provided a maxim for every occasion, the inventor who flew a kite in an electrical storm, the theorist who studied and held discussions with flies, the diplomat who made the British empire quake in her boots, and the man who stayed focused, calm, and in control during incendiary times.

Charismatic and intelligent, industrious and courageous, bold and innovative, articulate and outspoken, Benjamin Franklin was a maverick and a visionary. Embodying the hopes and aspirations of a young America, he helped parent a nation, nurture the independence of a revolutionary country, and foster the realization of a dream—a dream that with little else besides the clothes on one's back one could, through diligence and prudence, become a success.

—S.M. Wu
1995

Franklin's Epitaph

The Body
of
Benjamin Franklin
Printer
(Like the cover of an old book
Its contents torn out
And stript of its lettering and gilding)
Lies here, food for worms.
But the work shall not be lost
For it will (as he believed) appear once more
In a new and more elegant edition
Revised and corrected
by
The Author.

Written by Benjamin Franklin in 1728
when he was twenty-two years old.

1

Franklin's Plan of Conduct

THOSE WHO WRITE OF THE ART OF poetry teach us that if we would write what may be worth the reading, we ought always, before we begin, to form a regular plan and design of our piece: otherwise, we shall be in danger of incongruity. I am apt to think it is the same as to life. I have never fixed a regular design in life; by which means it has been a confused variety of different scenes. I am now entering upon a new one: let me, therefore, make some resolutions, and form some scheme of action, that, henceforth, I may live in all respects like a rational creature.

1. It is necessary for me to be extremely frugal for some time, till I have paid what I owe.

2. To endeavor to speak truth in every instance; to give nobody expectations that are not likely to be answered, but aim at sincerity in every word and action—the most amiable excellence in a rational being.

3. To apply myself industriously to whatever business I take in hand, and not divert my mind from my business by any foolish project of growing suddenly rich; for industry and patience are the surest means of plenty.

4. I resolve to speak ill of no man whatever, not even in a matter of truth; but rather by some means excuse the faults I hear charged upon others, and proper occasions speak all the good I know of everybody.

Early to bed and early to rise,

Makes a man healthy, wealthy, and wise.

A Letter to His Son

Dear Son:

I HAVE EVER HAD A PLEASURE IN OBTAINING any little anecdotes of my ancestors. You may remember the inquiries I made among the remains of my relations when you were with me in England, and the journey I undertook for that purpose. Imagining it may be equally agreeable to you to learn the circumstances of *my* life, many of which you are yet unacquainted with, and expecting the enjoyment of a few weeks' uninterrupted leisure in my present, country retirement, I sit down to write them for you. To which I have besides some other inducements. Having emerged from the poverty and obscurity in which I was born and bred, to a state of affluence and some degree of reputation in the world, and having gone so far through life with a considerable share of felicity, the conducing means I made use of, which with the blessing of God so well succeeded, my posterity may like to know, as they may find some of them suitable to their own situations, and therefore fit to be imitated.

That felicity, when I reflected on it, has induced me sometimes to say, that were it offered to my choice, I should have no objection to a repetition of the same life from its beginning, only asking the advantages authors have in a second edition to correct some faults of the first. So I might, besides correcting the faults, change some sinister accidents and events of it for others more favorable. But though this were denied, I should still accept the offer....

If you would not be forgotten

As soon as you are dead and rotten,

Either write things worth reading,

Or do things worth the writing.

Inventor

&

Scientist

"Most of the learning in use, is of no great use."

The Kite Experiment

*A*S FREQUENT MENTION IS MADE IN the newspapers from Europe, of the success of the Philadelphia experiment for drawing the electric fire from clouds by means of pointed rods of iron erected on high buildings, etc. it may be agreeable to the curious to be informed, that the same experiment has succeeded in Philadelphia, though made in a different and more easy manner, which anyone may try, as follows.

Make a small cross of two light strips of cedar, the arms so long as to reach to the four corners of a large thin silk handkerchief when extended; tie the corners of the handkerchief to the extremities of the cross, so you have the body of a kite; which being properly accommodated with a tail, loop and string, will rise in the air, like those made of paper; but this being of silk is fitter to bear the wet and wind of a thunder gust without tearing. To the top of the upright stick of the cross is to be fixed a very sharp pointed wire, rising a foot or more above the wood. To the end of the twine, near the hand, is to be tied a silk ribbon, and where the twine and the silk join, a key may be fastened. This kite is to be raised when a thunder gust appears to be coming on, and the person who holds the string must stand within a door, or window, or under some cover, so that the silk ribbon may not be wet; and care must be taken that the twine does not touch the frame of the door or window. As soon as any of the thunder clouds come over the kite, the pointed wire will draw the electric fire from them, and the kite, with all the twine, will be electrified, and the loose filaments of the twine will stand out every way, and be attracted by an approaching finger. And when the rain has wet the kite and twine, so that it can conduct the electric fire freely, you will find it stream out plentifully from the key on the approach of your knuckle. At this key the phial may be charged; and from electric fire thus obtained, spirits may be kindled, and all the other electric experiments be performed, which are usually done by the help of a rubbed glass globe or tube; and thereby the *sameness* of the electric matter with that of lightning completely demonstrated.

The morning daylight appears plainer When you put out your candle.

An Economical Project

*I*F IT SHOULD BE SAID THAT PEOPLE ARE APT to be obstinately attached to old customs, and that it will be difficult to induce them to rise before noon, consequently my discovery can be of little use, I answer *Nil desperandum.* I believe all who have commonsense, as soon as they have learnt from this paper that it is daylight when the sun rises, will contrive to rise with him, and, to complete the rest, I would propose the following regulations:

First. Let a tax be laid of a louis per window on every window that is provided with shutters to keep out the light of the sun.

Second. Let the same salutary operation of police be made use of, to prevent our burning candles, that inclined us last winter to be more economical in burning wood; that is, let guards be placed in the shops of the wax and tallow chandlers, and no family be permitted to be supplied with more than one pound of candles per week.

Third. Let guards also be posted to stop all the coaches, etc. that would pass the streets after sunset, except those of physicians, surgeons, and midwives.

Fourth. Every morning, as soon as the sun rises, let all the bells in every church be set ringing; and if that is not sufficient, let cannon be fired in every street, to wake the sluggards effectually, and make them open their eyes to see their true interest.

All the difficulty will be in the first two or three days after which the reformation will be as natural and easy as the present irregularity; for, *ce n'est que le premier pas qui coûte.* Oblige a man to rise at four in the morning, and it is more than probable he will go willingly to bed at eight in the evening; and, having had eight hours' sleep, he will rise more willingly at four in the morning following. But this sum of ninety-six millions and seventy-five thousand livres is not the whole of what may be saved by my economical project. You may observe that I have calculated upon only one half of the year, and much may be saved in the other, though the days are shorter. Besides, the immense stock of wax and tallow left unconsumed during the summer will probably make candles much cheaper for the ensuing winter, and continue them cheaper as long as the proposed reformation shall be supported....

Oil and Water

*I*N THESE EXPERIMENTS, ONE CIRCUMSTANCE struck me with particular surprise. This was the sudden, wide, and forcible spreading of a drop of oil on the face of the water, which I do not know that anybody has hitherto considered. If a drop of oil is put on a highly polished marble table, or on a looking glass that lies horizontally, the drop remains in its place, spreading very little. But, when put on water, it spreads instantly many feet round, becoming so thin as to produce the prismatic colors, for a considerable space, and beyond them so much thinner as to be invisible, except in its effect of smoothing the waves at a much greater distance. It seems as if a mutual repulsion between its particles took place as soon as it touched the water, and a repulsion so strong as to act on other bodies swimming on the surface, as straw, leaves, chips, etc., forcing them to recede every way from the drop, as from a center, leaving a large clear space. The quantity of this force, and the distance to which it will operate, I have not yet ascertained; but I think it is a curious inquiry, and I wish to understand whence it arises.

Now I imagine that the wind, blowing over water thus covered with a film of oil, cannot easily *catch* upon it, so as to raise the first wrinkles, but slides over it and leaves it smooth as it finds it. It moves a little the oil indeed, which being between it and the water, serves it to slide with, and prevents friction, as oil does between those parts of a machine that would otherwise rub hard together. Hence the oil dropped on the windward side of a pond proceeds gradually to leeward, as may be seen by the smoothness it carries with it, quite to the opposite side. For the wind being thus prevented from raising the first wrinkles, that I call the elements of waves, cannot produce waves, which are to be made by continually acting upon, and enlarging those elements, and thus the whole pond is calmed.

Totally therefore we might suppress the waves in any required place, if we could come at the windward place where they take their rise. This in the ocean can seldom if ever be done. But perhaps something may be done on particular occasions, to moderate the violence of the waves when we are in the midst of them, and prevent their breaking where that would be inconvenient.

For, when the wind blows fresh, there are continually rising on the back of every great wave a number of small ones, which roughen its surface, and give the wind hold, as it were, to push it with greater force. This hold is diminished, by preventing the generation of those small ones. And possibly too when a wave's surface is oiled, the wind in passing over it may rather in some degree press it down, and contribute to prevent its rising again, instead of promoting it.

This, as mere conjecture, would have little weight, if the apparent effects of pouring oil into the midst of waves were not considerable, and as yet not otherwise accounted for....

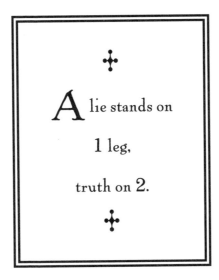

A lie stands on

1 leg,

truth on 2.

If thou wouldst live long, live well;
For folly and wickedness shorten life.

Death

takes

no

bribes.

Life and Death

A TOAD BURIED IN SAND WILL LIVE, it is said, till the sand becomes petrified, and then, being closed in the stone, it may live for we know not how many ages. The facts which are cited in support of this opinion are too numerous and too circumstantial not to deserve a certain degree of credit. As we are accustomed to see all the animals with which we are acquainted eat and drink, it appears to us difficult to conceive how a toad can be supported in such a dungeon; but if we reflect that the necessity of nourishment which animals experience in their ordinary state proceeds from the continual waste of their substance by perspiration, it will appear less incredible that some animals in a torpid state, perspiring less because they use no exercise, should have less need of aliment, and that others, which are covered with scales or shells, which stop perspiration, such as land and sea turtles, serpents, and some species of fish, should be able to subsist a considerable time without any nourishment whatever. A plant, with its flowers, fades and dies immediately if exposed to the air without having its root immersed in a humid soil, from which it may draw a sufficient quantity of moisture to supply that which exhales from its substance and is carried off continually by the air. Perhaps, however, if it were buried in quicksilver it might preserve for a considerable space of time its vegetable life, its smell, and color. If this be the case, it might prove a commodious method of transporting from distant countries those delicate plants which are unable to sustain the inclemency of the weather at sea, and which require particular care and attention. I have seen an instance of common flies preserved in a manner somewhat similar. They had been drowned in Madeira wine, apparently about the time when it was bottled in Virginia to be sent hither (to London). At the opening of one of the bottles at the house of a friend where I then was, three drowned flies fell into the first glass that was filled. Having heard it remarked that drowned flies were capable of being revived by the rays of the sun, I proposed making the experiment upon these. They were, therefore, exposed to the sun upon a sieve which had been employed to strain them out of the wine. In less than three hours two of them began by degrees to recover life. They commenced by some convulsive notions of the thighs, and at length they raised themselves upon their legs, wiped their eyes with their forefeet, beat and brushed their wings with their hind feet, and soon after began to fly, finding themselves in Old England, without knowing how they came thither. The third continued lifeless till sunset, when losing all hopes of him, he was thrown away.

I wish it were possible, from this instance, to invent a

method of embalming drowned persons in such a manner that they may be recalled to life at any period, however, distant; for having a very ardent desire to see and observe the state of America a hundred years hence, I should prefer to any ordinary death the being immersed in a cask of Madeira wine with a few friends till that time, to be then recalled to life by the solar warmth of my dear country! But since in all probability we live in an age too early and too near the infancy of science to hope to see such an art brought in our time to its perfection, I must for the present content myself with the treat which you are so kind as to promise me of the resurrection of a fowl or a turkey-cock.

> When death puts out our flame,
>
> the snuff will tell,
>
> If we were wax or tallow
>
> by the smell.
>
>

Philosopher

"Fear not death,

for the sooner we die,

The longer shall

we be immortal."

The Whistle

*I*N MY OPINION WE MIGHT ALL DRAW MORE good from [this world] than we do, and suffer less evil, if we would take care not to give too much for *whistles*. For to me it seems that most of the unhappy people we meet with are become so by neglect of that caution.

You ask what I mean? You love stories, and will excuse my telling one of myself.

When I was a child of seven years old, my friends, on a holiday, filled my pocket with coppers. I went directly to a shop where they sold toys for children; and being charmed with the sound of a *whistle*, that I met by the way in the hands of another boy, I voluntarily offered and gave all my money for one. I then came home, and went whistling all over the house, much pleased with my *whistle*, but disturbing all the family. My brothers, and sisters, and cousins, understanding the bargain I had made, told me I had given four times as much for it as it was worth; put me in mind what good things I might have bought with the rest of the money; and laughed at me so much for my folly, that I cried with vexation; and the reflection gave me more chagrin than the whistle gave me pleasure.

This, however, was afterwards of use to me, the impression continuing on my mind; so that often, when I was tempted to buy some unnecessary thing, I said to myself, "Don't give too much for the whistle"; and I saved my money.

As I grew up, came into the world, and observed the actions of men, I thought I met with many, very many, who *gave too much for the whistle.*

When I saw one too ambitious of court favor, sacrificing his time in attendance on levees, his repose, his liberty, his virtue, and perhaps his friends, to attain it, I have said to myself, "This man gives too much for his whistle."

When I saw another fond of popularity, constantly employing himself in political bustles, neglecting his own affairs, and ruining them by that neglect, "He pays, indeed," said I, "too much for his whistle."

If I knew a miser, who gave up every kind of comfortable living, all the pleasure of doing good to others, all the esteem of his fellow-citizens, and the joys of benevolent friendship, for the sake of accumulating wealth, "Poor man," said I, "you pay too much for your whistle."

When I met with a man of pleasure, sacrificing every laudable improvement of the mind, or of his fortune, to mere corporeal sensations, and ruining his health in their pursuit, "Mistaken man," said I, "you are providing pain for yourself, instead of pleasure; you give too much for your whistle."

If I see one fond of appearance, or fine clothes, fine

houses, fine furniture, fine equipages, all above his fortune, for which he contracts debts, and ends his career in prison, "Alas," say I, "he has paid dear, very dear, for his whistle."

When I see a beautiful, sweet-tempered girl married to an ill-natured brute of a husband, "What a pity," say I, "that she should pay so much for a whistle!"

In short, I conceive that great part of the miseries of mankind are brought upon them by the false estimates they have made of the value of things, and by their *giving too much for their whistles.*

Content and riches

Seldom meet together,

Riches take thou,

Contentment I had rather.

A h simple man!
When a boy
two precious jewels
were given thee,
Time, and good advice;
One thou hast lost,
and the other
thrown away.

The Ephemera:

AN EMBLEM OF HUMAN LIFE

YOU MAY REMEMBER, MY DEAR FRIEND, that when we lately spent that happy day in the delightful garden and sweet society of the Moulin Joly, I stopped a little in one of our walks, and stayed some time behind the company. We had been shown numberless skeletons of a kind of little fly, called an ephemera, whose successive generations, we were told, were bred and expired within the day. I happened to see a living company of them on a leaf, who appeared to be engaged in conversation. You know I understand all the inferior animal tongues. My too great application to the study of them is the best excuse I can give for the little progress I have made in your charming language. I listened through curiosity to the discourse of these little creatures; but as they, in their national vivacity, spoke three or four together, I could make but little of their conversation. I found, however, by some broken expressions that I heard now and then, they were disputing warmly on the merit of two foreign musicians, one a *cousin*, the other a *moscheto;* in which dispute they spent their time, seemingly as regardless of the shortness of life as if they had been sure of living a month. Happy people! thought I; you are certainly under a wise, just, and mild government, since you have no public grievances to complain of, nor any subject of contention but the perfections and imperfections of foreign music. I turned my head from them to an old gray-headed one, who was single on another leaf, and talking to himself. Being amused with his soliloquy, I put it down in writing, in hopes it will likewise amuse her to whom I am so much indebted for the most pleasing of all amusements, her delicious company and heavenly harmony.

"It was," said he, "the opinion of learned philosophers of our race, who lived and flourished long before my time, that this vast world, the Moulin Joly, could not itself subsist more than eighteen hours; and I think there was some foundation for that opinion, since, by the apparent motion of the great luminary that gives life to all nature, and which in my time has evidently declined considerably towards the ocean at the end of our earth, it must then finish its course, be extinguished in the waters that surround us, and leave the world in cold and darkness, necessarily producing universal death and destruction. I have lived seven of those hours, a great age, being no less than four hundred and twenty minutes of time. How very few of us continue so long! I have seen generations born, flourish, and expire. My present friends are the children and grandchildren of the friends of my youth, who are now, alas, no more! And I must soon follow them; for, by the course of nature, though still in health, I cannot expect to live above seven or eight minutes longer.

What now avails all my toil and labor in amassing honey-dew on this leaf, which I cannot live to enjoy! What the political struggles I have been engaged in for the good of my compatriot inhabitants of this bush, or my philosophical studies for the benefit of our race in general! for in politics what can laws do without morals? Our present race of ephemera will in a course of minutes become corrupt, like those of other and older bushes, and consequently as wretched. And in philosophy how small our progress! Alas! art is long, and life is short! My friends would comfort me with the idea of a name they say I shall leave behind me; and they tell me I have lived long enough to nature and to glory. But what will fame be to an ephemera who no longer exists? And what will become of all history in the eighteenth hour, when the world itself, even the whole Moulin Joly, shall come to its end and be buried in universal ruin?"

Dost thou love life?
then do not squander time;
For that's the stuff
life is made of.

L ost time
is never
found again.

T he sleeping fox
catches no poultry.
Up! up!

Fables

Fable I

A herd of cows had long afforded plenty of milk, butter, and cheese to an avaricious farmer, who grudged them the grass they subsisted on, and at length moved it to make money of the hay, leaving them to *shift for food* as they could, and yet still expected to *milk them* as before; but the cows, offended with his unreasonableness, resolved for the future *to suckle one another*.

Fable II

An eagle, King of Birds, sailing on his wings aloft over a farmer's yard, saw a cat there basking in the sun, *mistook it for a rabbit*, stooped, seized it, and carried it up into the air, *intending to prey on it*. The cat turning, set her claws into the eagle's breast; who, finding his mistake, opened his talons, and would have let her drop; but puss, unwilling to fall so far, held faster; and the eagle, to get rid of the inconvenience, found it necessary to *set her down where he took her up.*

Fable III

A lion's whelp was put on board a guinea ship bound to America as a present to a friend in that country: It was tame and harmless as a kitten, and therefore not confined, but suffered to walk about the ship at pleasure. A stately, full-grown English mastiff, belonging to the captain, despising the weakness of the young lion, frequently took its *food* by force, and often turned it out of its lodging box, when he had a mind to repose therein himself. The young lion nevertheless grew daily in size and strength, and the voyage being long, he became at last a more equal match for the mastiff; who continuing his insults, received a stunning blow from the lion's paw that fetched his skin over his ears, and deterred him from any future contest with such growing strength; regretting that he had not rather secured its friendship than provoked its enmity.

The Morals of Chess

THE GAME OF CHESS IS NOT MERELY an idle amusement. Several very valuable qualities of the mind, useful in the course of human life, are to be acquired or strengthened by it, so as to become habits, ready on all occasions. For life is a kind of chess, in which we often have points to gain, and competition or adversaries to contend with; and in which there is a vast variety of good and ill events, that are in some degree the effects of prudence or the want of it. By playing at chess, then, we may learn:

I. FORESIGHT, which looks a little into futurity, and considers the consequences that may attend an action; for it is continually occurring to the player, "If I move this piece, what will be the advantages or disadvantages of my new situation? What use can my adversary make of it to annoy me? What other moves can I make to support it, and to defend myself from his attacks?"

II. CIRCUMSPECTION, which surveys the whole chessboard, or scene of action; the relation of the several pieces and situations, the dangers they are respectively exposed to, the several possibilities of their aiding each other, the probability that the adversary may make this or that move, and attack this or the other piece, and what different means can be used to avoid his stroke, or turn its consequences against him.

III. CAUTION, not to make our moves too hastily. This habit is best acquired, by observing strictly the laws of the game; such as, *If you touch a piece, you must move it somewhere; if you set it down, you must let it stand.* And it is therefore best that these rules should be observed, as the game becomes thereby more the image of human life, and particularly of war; in which, if you have incautiously put yourself into a bad and dangerous position, you cannot obtain your enemy's leave to withdraw your troops, and place them more securely, but you must abide all the consequences of your rashness.

And *lastly,* we learn by chess the habit of not being discouraged by present appearances in the state of our affairs, the habit of hoping for a favorable change, and that of persevering in the search of resources.

The Art of Procuring
Pleasant Dreams

1. By eating moderately (as before advised for health's sake) less perspirable matter is produced in a given time; hence the bedclothes receive it longer before they are saturated, and we may therefore sleep longer before we are made uneasy by their refusing to receive any more.

2. By using thinner and more porous bedclothes, which will suffer the perspirable matter more easily to pass through them, we are less incommoded, such being longer tolerable.

3. When you are awakened by this uneasiness, and find you cannot easily sleep again, get out of bed, beat up and turn your pillow, shake the bedclothes well, with at least twenty shakes, then throw the bed open and leave it to cool; in the meanwhile, continuing undressed, walk about your chamber till your skin has had time to discharge its load, which it will do sooner as the air may be dried and colder.

When you begin to feel the cold air unpleasant, then return to your bed, and you will soon fall asleep, and your sleep will be sweet and pleasant. All the scenes presented to your fancy will be too of the pleasing kind. I am often as agreeably entertained with them, as by the scenery of an opera. If you happen to be too indolent to get out of bed, you may, instead of it, lift up your bedclothes with one arm and leg, so as to draw in a good deal of fresh air, and by letting them fall force it out again. This, repeated twenty times, will so clear them of the perspirable matter they have imbibed, as to permit your sleeping well for some time afterwards. But this latter method is not equal to the former.

Those who do not love trouble, and can afford to have two beds, will find great luxury in rising, when they wake in a hot bed, and going into the cool one. Such shifting of beds would also be of great service to persons ill of a fever, as it refreshes and frequently procures sleep. A very large bed, that will admit a removal so distant from the first situation as to be cool and sweet, may in a degree answer the same end....

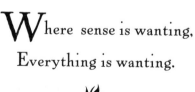

Where sense is wanting,

Everything is wanting.

Rules for Making Oneself a Disagreeable Companion

YOUR BUSINESS IS TO SHINE; THEREFORE, you must by all means prevent the shining of others, for their brightness may make yours the less distinguished. To this end:

1. If possible engross the whole discourse; and when other matter fails, talk much of yourself, your education, your knowledge, your circumstances, your successes in business, your victories in disputes, your own wise sayings and observations on particular occasions, etc., etc., etc.

2. If when you are out of breath, one of the company should seize the opportunity of saying something; watch his words, and, if possible, find somewhat either in his sentiment or expression, immediately to contradict and raise a dispute upon. Rather than fail, criticize even his grammar.

3. If another should be saying an indisputably good thing; either give no attention to it; or interrupt him; or draw away the attention of others; or, if you can guess what he would be at, be quick and say it before him; or, if he gets it said, and you perceive the company pleased with it, own it to be a good thing, and withal remark that it had been said by Bacon, Locke, Bayle, or some other eminent writer; thus you deprive him of the reputation he might have gained by it, and gain some yourself, as you hereby show your great reading and memory.

4. When modest men have been thus treated by you a few times, they will choose ever after to be silent in your company; then you may shine on without fear of a rival; rallying them at the same time for their dullness, which will be to you a new fund of wit.

Thus you will be sure to please *yourself.* The polite man aims at pleasing *others,* but you shall go beyond him even in that. A man can be present only in one company, but may at the same time be present in twenty. He can please only where he is, you wherever you are *not.*

Old Folks and Old Trees

AS *HAVING THEIR OWN WAY,* IS ONE OF the greatest comforts of life, to old people, I think their friends should endeavor to accommodate them in that, as well as in anything else. When they have long lived in a house, it becomes natural to them, they are almost as closely connected with it as the tortoise with his shell, they die if you tear them out of it. Old folks and old trees, if you remove them, tis ten to one that you kill them. So let our good old Sister be no more importuned on that head. We are growing old fast ourselves, and shall expect the same kind of indulgencies. If we give them, we shall have a right to receive them in our turn.

And as to her few fine things, I think she is in the right not to sell them and for the reasons she gives, that they will fetch but little. When that little is spent, they would be of no farther use to her; but perhaps the expectation of possessing them at her death, may make that person tender and careful of her, and helpful to her, to the amount of ten times their value. If so, they are put to the best use they possibly can be.

I hope you visit Sister as often as your affairs will permit, and afford her what assistance and comfort you can, in her present situation. *Old age, infirmities,* and *poverty* joined, are afflictions enough; the *neglect* and *slight* of friends and near relations, should never be added....

L,ove,

and

be loved.

A Tale

THERE WAS ONCE AN OFFICER, A WORTHY man, named Montrésor, who was very ill. His parish priest, thinking he would die, advised him to make his peace with God, so that he would be received into Paradise. "I don't feel much uneasiness on that score," said Montrésor; "for last night I had a vision which set me entirely at rest." "What vision did you have?" asked the good priest. "I was," he said, "at the Gate of Paradise with a crowd of people who wanted to enter. And St. Peter asked each of them what religion he belonged to. One answered, 'I am Roman Catholic.' 'Very well,' said St. Peter; 'come in, and take your place over there among the Catholics.' Another said he belonged to the Anglican Church. 'Very well,' said St. Peter; 'come in, and take your place among the Quakers.' Finally he asked me what my religion was. 'Alas!' I replied, 'Unfortunately, poor Jacques Montrésor belongs to none at all.' 'That's a pity,' said the Saint. 'I don't know where to put you but come in anyway; just find a place for yourself wherever you can.' "

Statesman

"Kings have long arms,
but Misfortune longer:
Let none think themselves
out of her reach."

How a Nation Acquires Wealth

THERE SEEM TO BE BUT THREE WAYS for a nation to acquire wealth. The first is by *war*, as the Romans did, in plundering their conquered neighbors. This is *robbery*. The second by *commerce*, which is generally *cheating*. The third by *agriculture*, the only *honest way*, wherein man receives a real increase of the seed thrown into the ground, in a kind of continual miracle, wrought by the hand of God in his favor, as a reward for his innocent life and his virtuous industry.

Great talkers,

little doers.

＊

Light purse,
heavy heart.

Necessity has no law;
Why? Because 'tis not
to be had without money.

Protective Duties on Imports and How They Work

SUPPOSE A COUNTRY, X, WITH THREE manufactures, as *cloth, silk, iron*, supplying three other countries, A, B, C, but is desirous of increasing the vent, and raising the price of cloth in favor of her own clothiers.

In order to do this, she forbids the importation of foreign cloth from A.

A, in return, forbids silks from X.
Then the silk-workers complain of a decay of trade.
And X, to content them, forbids silks from B.

B, in return, forbids iron ware from X.
Then the iron-workers complain of decay.
And X forbids the importation of iron from C.

C, in return, forbids cloth from X.
What is got by all these prohibitions?

Answer.—All four find their common stock of the enjoyments and conveniences of life diminished.

Those who in quarrels interpose,
Must often wipe a bloody nose.

Wars
bring
scars.

The Effects of War

I LAMENT WITH YOU THE PROSPECT OF A horrid war, which is likely to engage so great a part of mankind. There is little good gained, and so much mischief done generally, by wars, that I wish the imprudence of undertaking them was more evident to princes; in which case I think they would be less frequent. If I were counselor of the Empress of Russia, and found that she desired to possess some part of the dominions of the Grand Seignior, I should advise her to compute the annual taxes raised from that territory, and make him an offer of buying it, at the rate of paying for it at twenty years' purchase. And if I were his counselor, I should advise him to take the money and cede the dominion of that territory. For I am of opinion that a war to obtain it would cost her more than that sum, and the event uncertain, and that the defense of it will cost him as much, and not having embraced the offer, his loss is double. But to make and accept such an offer, these potentates should be both of them reasonable creatures, and free from the ambition of glory, which perhaps is too much to be supposed.

N ow I've a sheep
and a cow,
Everybody bids me
good morrow.

M ad Kings and mad bulls,
are not to be held
by treaties and packthread.

How to Make a
Great Empire a Small One

*A*N ANCIENT SAGE VALUED HIMSELF upon this, that, though he could not fiddle he knew how to make a great city of a little one. The science that I, a modern simpleton, am about to communicate, is the very reverse.

I address myself to all ministers who have the management of extensive dominions, which from their very greatness have become troublesome to govern, because the multiplicity of their affairs leaves no time for fiddling.

In the first place, gentlemen, you are to consider that a great empire, like a great cake, is most easily diminished at the edges. Turn your attention, therefore, first to your *remotest* provinces; that, as you get rid of them, the next may follow in order.

However peaceably your colonies have submitted to your government, shown their affection to your interests, and patiently borne their grievances, you are to suppose them *always inclined to revolt*, and treat them accordingly. Quarter troops among them, who by their insolence may provoke the rising of mobs, and by their bullets and bayonets suppress them. By this means, like the husband who uses his wife ill from suspicion, you may in time convert your suspicions into realities.

Remote provinces must have governors and judges to represent the royal person and execute everywhere the delegated parts of his office and authority. Your ministers know that much of the strength of government depends on the opinion of the people, and much of that opinion on the *choice of rulers* placed immediately over them. If you send them wise and good men for governors, who study the interests of the colonists, and advance their prosperity, they will think their king wise and good, and that he wishes the welfare of his subjects. If you send them learned and upright men for judges, they will think him a lover of justice. This may attach your provinces more to his government. You are therefore to be careful whom you recommend to those offices. If you can find prodigals who have ruined their fortunes, broken gamesters or stockjobbers, these may do well as governors; for they will probably be rapacious, and provoke the people by their extortions. Wrangling proctors and pettifogging lawyers, too, are not amiss; for they will be forever disputing and quarreling with their little Parliaments. If withal they should be ignorant, wrongheaded, and insolent, so much the better. Attorney's clerks and Newgate solicitors will do for chief justices, especially if they hold their places during your pleasure; and all will contribute to impress those ideas of your government that are proper for a people you would wish to renounce it.

To confirm these impressions and strike them deeper, whenever the injured come to the capital with complaints of maladministration, oppression, or injustice, *punish such suitors* with long delay, enormous expense and a final judgment in favor of the oppressor. This will have an admirable effect every way. The trouble of future complaints will be prevented, and governors and judges will be encouraged to further acts of oppression and injustice; and thence the people may become more disaffected, and at length desperate.

If when you are engaged in war, your colonies should vie in liberal aids of men and money against the common enemy, upon your simple requisition, and give far beyond their abilities, reflect that a penny taken from them by your power is more honorable to you than a pound presented by their benevolence; *despise therefore their voluntary grants*, and resolve to harass them with *novel taxes*. They will probably complain to your Parliament, that they are taxed by a body in which they have no representative and that this is contrary to common right. They will petition for redress. Let the Parliament flout their claims, reject their petitions, refuse even to suffer the reading of them, and treat the petitioners with the utmost contempt. Nothing can have a better effect in producing the alienation proposed; for, though many can forgive injuries, none ever forgave contempt.

Possibly, indeed, some of them might still comfort themselves, and say; "Though we have no property, we have yet something left that is valuable; we have constitutional *liberty, both of person and of conscience.* This King, these Lords, and these Commons, who it seems are too remote from us to know us, and feel for us, cannot take from us our Habeas Corpus right, or our right of trial by a jury of our neighbors; they cannot deprive us of the exercise of our religion, alter our ecclesiastical constitution, and compel us to be Papists, if they please, or Mahometans." To annihilate this comfort, begin by laws to perplex their commerce with infinite regulations, impossible to be remembered and observed; ordain seizures of their property for every failure; take away the trial of such property by jury, and give it to arbitrary judges of your own appointing, and of the lowest characters in the country, whose salaries and emoluments are to arise out of the duties or condemnations, and whose appointments are during pleasure. Then let there be a formal declaration of both houses, that opposition to your edicts is treason, and that persons suspected of treason in the provinces may, according to same obsolete law, be seized and sent to the metropolis of the empire for trial; and pass an act, that those there charged with certain other offenses shall be sent away in chains from their friends and country to be tried in the same manner for felony. Then erect a new court of Inquisition among them, accompanied by an armed force, with instructions to transport all such suspected persons; to be ruined by the expense, if they bring over evidences to prove their innocence, or be found guilty and hanged if they cannot afford it. And, lest the people should think you cannot possibly go any further, pass another solemn declaratory act, "that Kings, Lords, Commons had, have, and of right ought to have, full power and authority to make statutes of sufficient force and validity to bind the unrepresented provinces *in all cases whatsoever.* This will include spiritual with temporal, and, taken together, must operate wonderfully to your purpose; by convincing them that they are at present under a power something like that spoken of in the Scriptures, which can not only kill their bodies, but damn their souls to all eternity, by compelling them, if it pleases, to worship the Devil.

If you are told of *discontents* in your colonies, never believe that they are general, or that you have given occasion for them; therefore do not think of applying any remedy, or of changing any offensive measure. Redress no grievance, lest they should be encouraged to demand the redress of some other grievance. Grant no request that is just and reasonable, lest they should make another that is unreasonable. Take all your informations of the state of the colonies from your governors and officers in enmity with them. Encourage and reward these leasing-makers; secrete their lying accusations, lest they should be confuted; but act upon them as the clearest evidence; and believe nothing you hear from the friends of the people. Suppose all *their* complaints to be invented and promoted by a few factious demagogues, whom if you could catch and hang, all would be quiet. Catch and hang a few of them accordingly; and the blood of the martyrs shall work miracles in favor of your purpose.

Send armies into their country under pretense of protecting the inhabitants; but, instead of garrisoning the forts on their frontiers with those troops to prevent incursions, demolish those forts and order the troops into the heart of the country, that the savages may be encouraged to attack the frontiers, and that the troops may be protected by the inhabitants. This will seem to proceed from your *ill-will or your ignorance*, and contribute further to produce and strengthen an opinion among them that you are no longer fit to govern them.

Lastly, invest the *general of your army in the provinces* with great and unconstitutional powers, and free him from the control of even your own civil governors. Let him have troops enough under his command, with all the fortresses in his possession; and who knows but (like some provincial generals in the Roman empire, and encouraged by the universal discontent you have produced) he may take it into his head to set up for himself? If he should, and you have carefully practiced the few excellent rules of mine, take my word for it, all the provinces will immediately join him; and you will that day (if you have not done it sooner) get rid of the trouble of governing them, and all the plagues attending their commerce and connection from thenceforth and forever.

Be at war with your vices,

At peace with your neighbors,

And let every New Year

find you a better man.

The doors of wisdom

are never shut.

On Government

A N ANCIENT SAGE OF THE LAW SAYS: "The King can do no wrong, for, if he doeth wrong, he is not the King." And in another place: "When the King doth justice, he is God's vicar; but when he doth unjustly, he is the agent of the Devil." The politeness of the later times has given a softer turn to the expression. It is now said: *The King can do no wrong, but his ministers may.* In allusion to this the Parliament of 1641 declared they made war against the King for the King's service. But his Majesty affirmed that such a distinction was absurd; though, by the way, his own creed contained a greater absurdity, for he believed he had an authority from God to oppress the subjects whom by the same authority he was obliged to cherish and defend. Aristotle calls all princes tyrants, from the moment they set up an interest different from that of their subjects; and this is the only definition he gives us of tyranny. Our own country-men before cited and the sagacious Greek both agree on this point, that a governor who acts contrary to the ends of gov-ernment loses the title bestowed on him at his institution. It would be highly improper to give the same name to things of different qualities or that produce different effects. Matter, while it communicates heat, is generally called fire, but when the flames are extinguished the appellation is changed. Sometimes indeed the same sound serves to express things of a contrary nature, but that only denotes a defect or poverty in the language.

A wicked prince imagines that the crown receives a new luster from absolute power, whereas every step he takes to obtain it is a forfeiture of the crown.

His conduct is as foolish as it is detestable; he aims at glory and power, and treads the path that leads to dishonor and contempt; he is a plague to his country, and deceives himself.

During the inglorious reigns of the Stuarts (except a part of Queen Anne's), it was a perpetual struggle between them and the people: those endeavoring to subvert, and those bravely opposing the subverters of liberty. What were the consequences? One lost his life on the scaffold, another was banished. The memory of all of them stinks in the nostrils of every true lover of his country; and their history stains with indelible blots the English annals.

The reign of Queen Elizabeth furnishes a beautiful contrast. All her views centered in one object, which was the public good. She made it her study to gain the love of her subjects, not by flattery or little soothing arts, but by rendering them substantial favors. It was far from her policy to encroach on their privileges; she augmented and secured them.

And it is remarked to her eternal honor, that the acts presented to her for her royal approbation (forty or fifty of a session of Parliament) were signed without examining any farther than the titles. This wise and good Queen only reigned for her people, and knew that it was absurd to imagine they would promote anything contrary to their own interests, which she so studiously endeavored to advance. On the other hand, when this Queen asked money of the Parliament they frequently gave her more than she demanded, and never inquired how it was disposed of, except for form's sake, being fully convinced she would not employ it but for the general welfare. Happy princes, happy people! What harmony, what mutual confidence! Seconded by the hearts and purses of her subjects, she crushed the exorbitant power of Spain, which threatened destruction to England and chains to all Europe. That monarchy has ever since pined under the stroke, so that now, when we send a man-of-war or two to the West Indies, it puts her into such a panic fright that if the galleons can steal home she sings *Te Deum* as for a victory.

This is a true picture of government; its reverse is *tyranny*.

He that won't be counselled,

can't be helped.

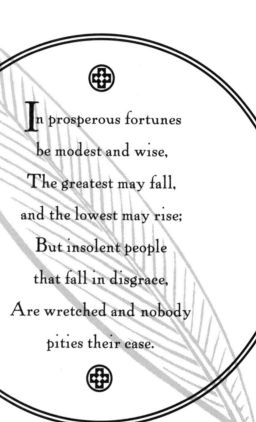

In prosperous fortunes
be modest and wise,
The greatest may fall,
and the lowest may rise;
But insolent people
that fall in disgrace,
Are wretched and nobody
pities their case.

On Sending Felons to
America

WE MAY ALL REMEMBER THE TIME when our Mother Country, as a mark of her parental tenderness, emptied her jails into our habitations, *"for the better peopling,"* as she expressed it, "of the colonies." It is certain that no due returns have yet been made for these valuable consignments. We are therefore much in her debt on that account; and, as she is of late clamorous for the payment of all we owe her, and some of our debts are of a kind not so easily discharged, I am for doing however what is in our power. It will show our good will as to the rest. The felons she planted among us have produced such an amazing increase, that we are now enabled to make ample remittance in the same commodity. And since the Wheelbarrow Law is not found effectually to reform them, and many of our vessels are idle through her restraints on our trade, why should we not employ those vessels in transporting the felons to Britain?

I was led into this thought by perusing the copy of a petition to Parliament, which fell lately by accident into my hands. It has no date, but I conjecture from some circumstances, that it must have been about the year 1767 or '68. (It seems, if presented, it had no effect, since the Act passed.) I imagine it may not be unacceptable to your readers, and therefore transcribe it for your paper; viz.

To the Honorable Knights,
Citizens, and Burgesses of Great Britain,
in Parliament assembled,

THE PETITION OF B. F.,
AGENT FOR THE PROVINCE OF
PENNSYLVANIA;
MOST HUMBLY SHOWETH;

That the transporting of felons from England to the plantations in America, is, and hath long been, a great grievance to the said plantations in general.

That the said felons, being landed in America, not only continue their evil practices to the annoyance of his majesty's good subjects there, but contribute greatly to corrupt the morals of the servants and poorer people among whom they are mixed.

That many of the said felons escape from the servitude to which they were destined, into other colonies, where their condition is not known; and, wandering at large from one populous town to another, commit many burglaries, robberies, and murders, to the great terror of the people; and occasioning heavy charges for apprehending and securing such felons, and bringing them to justice.

That your petitioner humbly conceives the easing one part of the British Dominions of their felons, by burdening another part with the same felons, cannot increase the common happiness of his Majesty's subjects, and that therefore the trouble and expense of transporting them is upon the whole altogether useless.

That your petitioner, nevertheless, observes with extreme concern in the votes of Friday last, that leave is given to bring in a bill for extending to Scotland, the Act made in the 4th year in the reign of King George the First, whereby the aforesaid grievances are, as he understands, to be greatly increased by allowing Scotland also to transport its felons to America.

Your petitioner therefore humbly prays, in behalf of Pennsylvania, and the other plantations in America, that the House would take the premises into consideration, and in their great wisdom and goodness repeal all Acts, and Clauses of Acts, for transporting of felons; or, if this may not at present be done, that they would at least reject the proposed bill for extending the said Acts to Scotland; or, if it be thought fit to allow of such extension, that then the said extension may be carried further, and the plantations be also, by an equitable clause in the same bill, permitted to transport their felons to Scotland.

And your petitioner, as in duty bound, shall pray, etc.

This petition, as I am informed, was not received by the House, and the Act passed.

On second thoughts, I am of opinion, that besides employing our own vessels, as above proposed, every English ship arriving in our ports with goods for sale, should be obliged to give bond, before she is permitted to trade, engaging that she will carry back to Britain at least one felon for every fifty tons of her burden. Thus we shall not only discharge sooner our debts, but furnish our old friends with the means on "better peopling," and with more expedition, their promising new Colony of Botany Bay.

An innocent plowman is more worthy than a vicious prince.

An Address to the Public from the Pennsylvania Society for Promoting the Abolition of Slavery, and the Relief of Free Negroes Unlawfully Held in Bondage

*I*T IS WITH PECULIAR SATISFACTION we assure the friends of humanity, that, in prosecuting the design of our association, our endeavors have proved successful far beyond our most sanguine expectations.

Encouraged by this success, and by the daily progress of that luminous and benign spirit of liberty, which is diffusing itself throughout the world, and humbly hoping for the continuance of the divine blessing on our labors, we have ventured to make an important addition to our original plan, and do therefore earnestly solicit the support and assistance of all who can feel the tender emotions of sympathy and compassion, or relish the exalted pleasure of beneficence.

Slavery is such an atrocious debasement of human nature, that its very extirpation, if not performed with solicitous care, may sometimes open a source of serious evils.

The unhappy man, who has long been treated as a brute animal, too frequently sinks beneath the common standard of the human species. The galling chains, that bind his body, do also fetter his intellectual faculties, and impair the social affections of his heart. Accustomed to move like a mere machine, by the will of a master, reflection is suspended; he has not the power of choice; and reason and conscience have but little influence over his conduct, because he is chiefly governed by the passion of fear. He is poor and friendless; perhaps worn out by extreme labor, age, and disease.

Under such circumstances, freedom may often prove a misfortune to himself, and prejudicial to society.

Attention to emancipated black people, it is therefore to be hoped, will become a branch of our national policy; but, as far as we contribute to promote this emancipation, so far that attention is evidently a serious duty incumbent on us, and which we mean to discharge to the best of our judgment and abilities.

To instruct, to advise, to qualify those who have been restored to freedom, for the exercise and enjoyment of civil liberty, to promote in them habits of industry, to furnish them with employments suited to their age, sex, talents, and other circumstances, and to procure their children an education calculated for their future situation in life; these are the great outlines of the annexed plan, which we have adopted, and which we conceive will essentially promote the public good, and the happiness of these our hitherto too much neglected fellow-creatures.

A plan so extensive cannot be carried into execution without considerable pecuniary resources, beyond the present ordinary funds of the Society. We hope much from the generosity of enlightened and benevolent freemen, and will gratefully receive any donations or subscriptions for this purpose, which may be made to our treasurer, James Starr, or to James Pemberton, chairman of our committee of correspondence.

Signed, by the order of the Society.

B. Franklin, *President*

All blood is alike ancient.

Extracts from
Poor Richard's
Almanac

"Who is wise?

He that learns from everyone.

Who is powerful?

He that governs his passions.

Who is rich?

He that is content.

Who is that?

Nobody."

He has changed his one-eyed horse for a blind one.

❖

Suspicion may be no fault,

But showing it may be a great one.

❖

Great beauty, great strength, and great riches,

Are really and truly of no great use;

A light heart exceeds all.

❖

Take counsel in wine, but resolve afterwards in water.

❖

Since thou art not sure of a minute,

Throw away not an hour.

❖

In other men we faults can spy,

And blame the mote that dims their eye;

Each little speck and blemish find;

To our own stronger errors blind.

❖

The heart of a fool is in his mouth,
But the mouth of a wiseman is in his heart.

Visits should be short like a winter's day,
Lest you're too troublesome hasten away.

When there's marriage without love,
There will be love without marriage.

He does not possess wealth, it possesses him.

If what most men admire, they would despise,
'Twould look as if mankind were growing wise.

Don't throw stones at your neighbors,
If your own windows are glass.

The sun never repents of the good he does,
Nor does he ever demand a recompense.

He that speaks much, is much mistaken.

He that would live in peace & at ease,
Must not speak all he knows, nor judge all he sees.

The man who with undaunted toils,
Sails unknown seas to unknown soils,
With various wonders feasts his sight:
What stranger wonders does he write?

Up, sluggard, and waste not life;
In the grave will be sleeping enough.

Experience keeps a dear school,
Yet fools will learn in no other.

A true friend is the best possession.

Hide not your talents, they for use were made.
What's a sun-dial in the shade!

Tis hard (but glorious) to be poor and honest;
An empty sack can hardly stand upright;
But if it does, 'tis a stout one!

The tongue is ever turning to the aching tooth.

He that cannot bear with other people's passions,
Cannot govern his own.

Glass, china, and reputation, are easily cracked,
And never well mended.

What's more valuable than gold?
Diamonds.
Than diamonds?
Virtue.

'Tis a strange forest that has no rotten wood in it.
And a strange kindred that all are good in it.

Life with fools consists in drinking;
With the wise man living's thinking.

Clean your finger, before you point at my spots.

The old man has given all to his son:
O fool! to undress thyself before thou art going to bed.

Anoint a villain and he'll stab you,
Stab him and he'll anoint you.

❖

I never saw an oft-transplanted tree,
Nor yet an oft-removed family,
That throve so well as those that settled be.

❖

One today, is worth two tomorrow.

❖

The fool hath made a vow, I guess,
Never to let the fire have peace.

❖

Hot things, sharp things, sweet things, cold things
All rot the teeth, and make them look like old things.

❖

He that is rich need not live sparingly,

And he that can live sparingly need not be rich.

Since I cannot govern my own tongue,

Though within my own teeth,

How can I hope to govern the tongues of others?

Each year one vicious habit rooted out,

In time might make the worst man good throughout.

Trouble springs from idleness; toil from ease.

Sin is not hurtful because it is forbidden

But it is forbidden because it's hurtful.

Nor is a duty beneficial because it is commanded,

But it is commanded, because it's beneficial.

When the well's dry, we know the worth of water.

Monkeys warm with envious spite,
Their most obliging friends will bite;—
And, fond to copy human ways,
Practice new mischiefs all their days.

An ounce of wit that is bought,
Is worth a pound that is taught.

Many complain of their memory,
Few of their judgment.

Empty free-booters covered with scorn:
They went out for wealth, and come ragged and torn,
As the ram went for wool, and was sent back shorn.

A slip of the foot you may soon recover:
But a slip of the tongue you may never get over.

Tim was so learned,
That he could name a horse in nine languages;
So ignorant, that he bought a cow to ride on.

Youth is pert and positive,
Age modest and doubting:
So ears of corn when young and light,
Stand bolt upright,
But hang their heads when weighty, full, and ripe.

Hear no ill of a friend, nor speak any of an enemy.

He that builds before he counts the cost,

Acts foolishly;

And he that counts before he builds,

Finds he did not count wisely.

Don't think so much of your own cunning,

As to forget other men's:

A cunning man is overmatched

By a cunning man and a half.

Do not do that which you would not have known.

When a friend deals with a friend

Let the bargain be clear and well penned,

That they may continue friends to the end.

Act uprightly, and despise calumny;

Dirt may stick to a mud wall,

But not to polished marble.

A full belly makes a dull brain:

The Muses starve in a cook's shop.

Rob not God, nor the poor, lest thou ruin thyself;

The eagle snatcht a coal from the altar,

But it fired her nest.

Learning to the studious;

Riches to the careful;

Power to the bold;

Heaven to the virtuous.

If you desire many things,
Many things will seem but a few.

Where there is hunger, law is not regarded;
And where law is not regarded, there will be hunger.

Of learned fools I have seen ten times ten,
Of unlearned wise men I have seen a hundred.

To whom thy secret thou dost tell,
To him thy freedom thou dost sell.

Thou canst not joke an enemy into a friend;
But thou may'st a friend into an enemy.

An open foe may prove a curse;
But a pretended friend is worse.

A long life may not be good enough,
But a good life is long enough.

If you would reap praise you must sow the seeds,
Gentle words and useful deeds.

A brother may not be a friend,
But a friend will always be a brother.

Poverty wants some things,
Luxury many things,
Avarice all things.

Do me the favor to deny me at once.

※

Here comes the orator! with his flood of words,
And his drop of reason.

※

Wink at small faults; remember thou hast great ones.

※

Reader, farewell, all happiness attend thee:
May each New Year better and richer find thee.